Minneapolis St. Paul

A Photo Tour of the Twin Cities

—— by Gregg Felsen ——

Adventure Publications, Inc.

Cambridge, Minnesota

Dedication

This book is dedicated to my father, Arthur Felsen, whose legacy of friendship, generosity, and love for life are remembered by all who knew him.

Credits

Cover photos by Gregg Felsen

Photos by Gregg Felsen

Cover and book design by Jonathan Norberg

10 9 8 7 6 5 4 3 2 1

Copyright 2008 by Gregg Felsen
Published by Adventure Publications, Inc.
820 Cleveland St. S
Cambridge, MN 55008
1-800-678-7006
www.adventurepublications.net

ISBN-13: 978-1-59193-082-2
ISBN-10: 1-59193-082-0

Minneapolis St. Paul

A Photo Tour of the Twin Cities

Introduction

The Minneapolis-St. Paul metropolitan area is the hub of culture, entertainment and commerce in the upper Midwest. Its unique urban landscape blends modern skylines and historic architecture against a breathtaking natural backdrop of rivers, lakes and green space.

Within 10 miles of downtown Minneapolis, the 14,000-acre Minnesota Valley National Wildlife Refuge provides one of the few places in the nation where bald eagles, coyotes and beavers are virtually next-door neighbors to more than 3 million people. In a perfect example of Twin Cities' diversity, refuge headquarters is located just one mile from the Mall of America in Bloomington, the country's largest retail and entertainment complex.

Across the Mississippi River in St. Paul, Historic Fort Snelling—a restored 1820s military outpost—offers yet another perspective of Twin Cities life. History also comes alive in the hallowed halls of the State Capitol, Fitzgerald Theater and Landmark Center. Yet just minutes from any of these destinations, you can watch the Minnesota Wild battle NHL hockey rivals in the state-of-the-art Xcel Energy Center or take in a concert or theatrical performance at a variety of venues.

Of course, this is only part of the ambiance. The Twin Cities are home to one of the largest public research universities in the country, the University of Minnesota, along with numerous other public and private educational institutions. The area is also a world leader in industry, technology and health care.

And then there's the people—diverse, yet similar in their warmth and passion for life. There are more golfers per capita here than anywhere in the country, and only New York can boast more theater seats per person. Thousands enjoy the expansive network of trails for hiking, cross-country skiing and mountain biking. Plus, with more than 1,000 lakes and four major rivers in the metro area, water-based recreation such as fishing, boating, swimming and canoeing is a major part of life.

Add it together and it's no wonder the area is consistently ranked one of the best places to live in the United States. Whether you come seeking music, museums, theatrical productions and restaurants or sports, parks and a slice of American history, you'll find it in the Twin Cities. It's all here, from the hip nightlife of Uptown to the serenity of a quiet sunrise on a Mississippi backwater.

Note: A directory of sites and resources begins on page 140.

Fascinating Facts About the Twin Cities

- The Twin Cities encompasses a 7-county metro area that includes 188 cities and townships, collectively forming the country's 16th-largest metropolitan area.

- Minneapolis and St. Paul are not "identical twins." With its heavy influence of late-Victorian architecture, St. Paul is considered the last of the country's Eastern cities. Minneapolis has been called the first city of the American West for its broad boulevards, grid-like layout and modern architecture.

- Both Minneapolis and St. Paul have extensive skyway systems appreciated by all in the winter. The Minneapolis system spans 7 miles, allowing access to 52 blocks. St. Paul's covers 5 miles, linking nearly every downtown building.

- Established in 1965, the Children's Theatre Company in Minneapolis is North America's largest professional theater company specifically for young people.

- Together, Minneapolis and St. Paul have more than 300 parks and open spaces, with over 25 miles of groomed cross-country ski trails.

- Minneapolis' Hubert H. Humphrey Metrodome is the world's only stadium to host all of the following: an NFL Super Bowl, two MLB World Series and an All-Star Game, and two NCAA Men's Final Four Basketball Championships.

- Summer brings an average of 13 days in the 90s. Winter usually delivers 30 days with below-zero temperatures. A typical July day sees a high of 83 and low of 63. In January, the average dips to a high of 22 and low of 4 degrees.

- On average, the Twin Cities' receives from 53 to 70 inches of snowfall each year. The record is 98.6 inches, set in the winter of 1983-'84.

- Major corporations calling the Twin Cities home include 3M, Best Buy, Cargill, General Mills, Land O'Lakes, Northwest Airlines and Target.

- The Mississippi River is the Twin Cities' most famous waterway, but it is only part of the story. There are approximately 1,003 lakes in the 7-county metro area, along with other scenic rivers such as the Minnesota, Rum and St. Croix. These waters support some of the state's finest fishing and boating opportunities.

50th & France

Located at the border of Edina and Minneapolis, this upscale business neighborhood is home to more than 175 shops, restaurants and services, from spas and clothing to an art-house movie theater.

Alexander Ramsey House

Located in St. Paul's Irvine Park neighborhood, the 16-room house is one of the country's best preserved Victorian homes. Alexander Ramsey served as Minnesota governor, U.S. Senator and Secretary of War.

American Swedish Institute

This elaborate, 33-room French Châteauesque-style mansion is home to the American Swedish Institute, the largest and oldest museum of Swedish-American culture in the United States. Swedish immigrant and newspaper publisher Swan J. Turnblad built the house at the turn of the century and founded the institute in 1929.

Back to the 50s

Sponsored by the Minnesota Street Rod Association since 1964 and held at the Minnesota State Fair grounds, this annual 3-day event in June attracts more than 11,500 vintage vehicles and 100,000 spectators. It is the second-largest car show of its kind in the world.

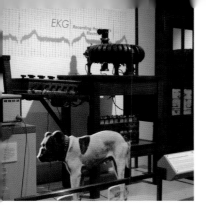

Bakken Museum

Medtronic co-founder Earl E. Bakken, inventor of the first wearable transistorized cardiac pacemaker, founded this Minneapolis museum, which focuses on the historical role of electricity and magnetism in science and medicine. Exhibits include the popular multimedia Frankenstein display.

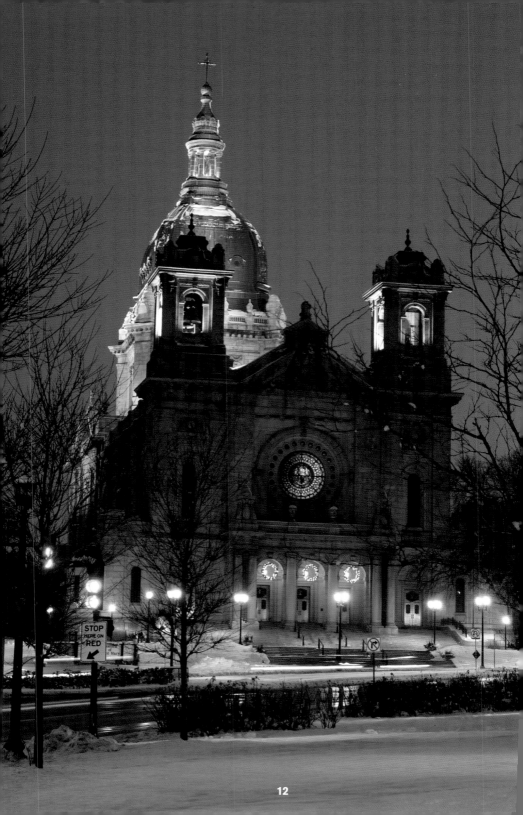

Basilica of St. Mary

This masterpiece of Beaux Arts Modern Renaissance architecture was the vision of Archbishop John Ireland and French Architect Emmanuel Masqueray, with construction beginning in 1907. It features a cavernous, vaulted 82-by-140-foot nave and 60 stained glass windows.

Minneapolis skyline from the Stone Arch Bridge

Bell Museum of Natural History

Originally named The Museum of Natural History at the University of Minnesota, the facility was renamed in 1966 to honor James Ford Bell, the founder of General Mills. The university museum features dozens of renowned diorama exhibits depicting Minnesota's natural habitats and animals, as well as a popular hands-on "Touch and See" room.

Biking

Among the many popular bicycle routes in the Twin Cities are the Gateway Trail, the Minneapolis Grand Rounds and the Luce Line Trail. The 18-mile Gateway Trail runs from St. Paul to Stillwater. As the only urban national scenic byway, the 50-mile Minneapolis Grand Rounds curves through the heart of the city. The 63-mile Luce Line Trail travels along mixed-surface trails from Plymouth to west-central Minnesota.

Block E

Once a haven for bars, pool halls and crime, Block E in downtown Minneapolis has been transformed into an entertainment zone that includes restaurants, shops, a 15-screen movie theater and a fashionable five-star hotel.

Boom Island

Part of the historic Minneapolis riverfront district, Boom Island's 25 acres include a boat launch, docks, promenade, playground, walking paths, and picnic and shelter areas. Riverfront cruises on the historic *Minneapolis Queen* are available here as well.

Cafesjian's Carousel

For more than half a century, this colorful, hand-carved wooden carousel was a beloved Minnesota State Fair attraction. Former West Publishing owner and philanthropist Gerard L. Cafesjian financially led the charge to restore the old ride, now located at St. Paul's Como Park.

Canterbury Park

Minnesota's only pari-mutuel horse-racing facility
features live thoroughbred and quarter horse
events. Located in Shakopee, Canterbury Park also
offers daily simulcast racing from America's top
tracks as well as 24-hour blackjack and a variety of
poker games.

Carlos Avery Wildlife Management Area

Named for Minnesota's first conservation commissioner, Carlos Avery covers nearly 25,000 acres of wildlife habitat in Anoka and Chisago counties. The area attracts some 100 bird species, including great blue herons, Canadian geese, sandhill cranes, wild swans and various birds of prey. Public hunting and trapping is allowed.

Cathedral of St. Paul

Atop Summit Hill overlooking the State Capitol and downtown St. Paul, this Mother Church of the Archdiocese of St. Paul and Minneapolis is modeled after St. Peter's in Rome. The cathedral features six chapels and a 175-foot-high dome.

Centennial Lakes Park

Edina's oasis of pond and greenery offers year-round entertainment on or near the 10-acre lake, including remote control sailboat races, concerts, fishing, paddleboat rides and ice skating, as well as croquet and lawn bowling courts and a putting course.

Chanhassen Dinner Theatres

More than 9 million guests have attended productions at the Chanhassen Dinner Theatres, the country's largest professional dinner theater with multiple stages under one roof. The 90,000-square-foot facility has staged performances of Broadway blockbusters such as *Cats*, *Grease* and *Les Misérables*.

Children's Theatre Company

Often considered the nation's premier children's theater, the Tony Award-winning CTC is among the 10 largest non-profit theaters in America.

Como Zoo

St. Paul's free-admission zoo is home to more than 250 animals, including lions, tigers, giraffes, gorillas and polar bears. The zoo is open 365 days a year. The Sparky the Sea Lion Show is a popular attraction during the summer months.

◄ Como-Harriet Streetcar Line
Three restored electric streetcars transport passengers back in time along a 1-mile, 15-minute breezy ride from the Linden Hills Station at Lake Harriet to the southeas shore of Lake Calhoun. The streetcars run from early May through mid-December.

epot Ice Rink

A bustling train depot for over 70 years, the former Milwaukee Road Depot is currently home to a popular seasonal indoor ice skating venue and Renaissance by Marriott hotel. *USA Today* calls the rink "one of the top 10 places in the United States to ice skate." The rink is open from late November through late March.

Dinkytown

Tucked north of the University of Minnesota's East Bank campus, Dinkytown includes assorted restaurants, bars, shops and student housing. Known for decades as the place to go for some of the city's best music, Dinkytown was once home to Bob Dylan.

lingson Car Museum

An easy 24-mile drive from downtown Minneapolis, the Ellingson Car Museum features an ever-changing assortment of more than 100 vintage vehicles on display and for sale. Exhibits include 1920s and 1930s American and European cars, muscle cars, even the "General Lee"—one of the famous orange 1969 Dodge Chargers made for *The Dukes of Hazzard* TV series.

LET NATURE BE YOUR TEACHER

Eloise Butler Wildflower Garden and Bird Sanctuary

Composed of almost 14 acres of woodlands, wetlands and prairies, this is the oldest public wildflower garden in the United States. In 1907, high school botany teacher Eloise Butler helped establish the Minneapolis garden, which includes 500 varieties of wildflowers and 140 different kinds of migratory birds.

Fitzgerald Theater

St. Paul's oldest surviving theater is now home to Garrison Keillor's *Prairie Home Companion* radio program. The 1,058-seat theater—with its two-story balcony and near-perfect acoustics and sight lines—was renamed in 1994 for novelist and St. Paul native son F. Scott Fitzgerald.

◄ Fort Snelling National Cemetery

Originally established in 1870 and formally dedicated as a national cemetery in 1939, the 463-acre cemetery contains the remains of more than 180,000 veterans and eligible survivors of veterans.

Foshay Tower

Modeled after the Washington Monument, the Foshay Tower was the first skyscraper west of the Mississippi River and the tallest building in Minneapolis until 1972. Six weeks after Wilber Foshay's building opened in 1929, the stock market crashed, sending Foshay's public utilities empire into receivership.

Golfing

Minnesota has more golfers per capita than any other state in America and the Twin Cities area has more than 200 courses. Twin Cities greens have hosted numerous professional men's, women's, senior and pro-am tournaments.

Grand Rounds National Scenic Byway

The Grand Rounds is a 50.1-mile-long system of roadways, paths and trails that encircles the city of Minneapolis. Divided into seven districts (Downtown Riverfront, Mississippi River, Minnehaha, Chain of Lakes, Theodore Wirth, Victory Memorial and Northeast), the Grand Rounds is the country's longest continuous system of public urban parkways and passes by some of the city's most beautiful neighborhoods, lakes, waterfalls, churches and museums.

Guthrie Theater

Founded by Anglo-Irish theatrical director and playwright Sir William Tyrone Guthrie, the Guthrie was modeled after the Stratford Theatre in Warwickshire, England. The Guthrie opened its 44th season in 2006 at a new 280,000-square-foot, 3-theater blue building located in the historic Mill District.

Harriet Island

Named after temperance reformer and suffragette Harriet Bishop, who was St. Paul's first school teacher, Harriet Island was given to the city in 1900 as a public recreation area. Across the Wabasha Street Bridge from downtown St. Paul, the island includes the Moderne-style pavilion designed by Clarence W. Wigington, the country's first black municipal architect.

Historic Fort Snelling ➤

Once the U.S. Army's most isolated military outpost, Fort Snelling was built in the 1820s on a bluff overlooking the confluence of the Mississippi and Minnesota rivers. Each year, some 500,000 people visit Fort Snelling, where staffers dressed in period costumes as soldiers, officers, cooks and tradesmen demonstrate crafts, recreate everyday chores and practice military drills.

Historic Murphy's Landing

Named for Major Richard Murphy, a government Indian agent during the 1850s, Murphy's Landing is an 88-acre living history museum located along the Minnesota River near Shakopee. Exhibits, including 44 period buildings, show what life was like for settlers on America's western frontier.

Iolidazzle

Four nights a week between Thanksgiving and Christmas, this festive
parade along Nicollet Mall in downtown Minneapolis celebrates the holiday
season with colorful floats, music, celebrity guests and fairy tale characters.

Hubert H. Humphrey Metrodome

Since opening in 1982, the Metrodome has been home to professional and collegiate sports including Minnesota's Twins, Vikings and University of Minnesota Golden Gophers. It has hosted the Super Bowl (1992), Major League Baseball's All-Star Game (1985), two World Series (1987, 1991), two NCAA Men's Basketball Championship Final Fours (1992, 2001) and numerous concerts, high school athletic championships and other events.

Jackson Street Roundhouse

Built in 1907 by the Great Northern Railroad, the roundhouse was one of the last fully functioning railroad steam engine and rolling stock maintenance shops. The Minnesota Transportation Museum opened the Jackson Street Roundhouse as a museum in 1999.

James J. Hill House

Legendary railroad magnate James J. Hill's five-story mansion on
Summit Avenue overlooks downtown St. Paul and the Mississippi
River. Built to Hill's exacting specifications, the 36,000-square-
foot red sandstone residence features 42 rooms, 13 bathrooms,
22 fireplaces and a two-story skylit art gallery.

John H. Stevens House

Built in 1849, this simple wooden home became the hub of a new
city. This was where citizens first suggested the name Minneapolis,
and Colonel John Stevens' house also served as the city's first
courthouse and one-room schoolhouse.

Jonathan Padelford ➤

One of the few authentic sternwheel vessels still in
operation, the *Jonathan Padelford* is the flagship
of four authentic riverboat replicas that cruise the
Mississippi River from early May through October.

Lake Calhoun

Named for vice president John C. Calhoun, who authorized the construction of Fort Snelling, this is the largest in Minneapolis' Chain of Lakes. Popular attractions at Lake Calhoun include biking and walking trails, three public beaches and two fishing docks, and activities such as windsurfing and ice fishing.

Lake Harriet

The lake's beautiful south Minneapolis setting and free summer band shell concerts attract hundreds of thousands of visitors a year. Lake Harriet is also popular with swimmers, sailors, anglers, canoeists, bicyclists, skaters, walkers and runners.

Minneapolis skyline from Lake Calhoun

Lake Harriet-Lyndale Park Rose Garden

Established in 1907/1908 and the second-oldest public rose garden in America, this 1.5-acre garden contains more than 3,000 roses of over 250 varieties. During the peak season, the garden can contain as many as 60,000 blooms.

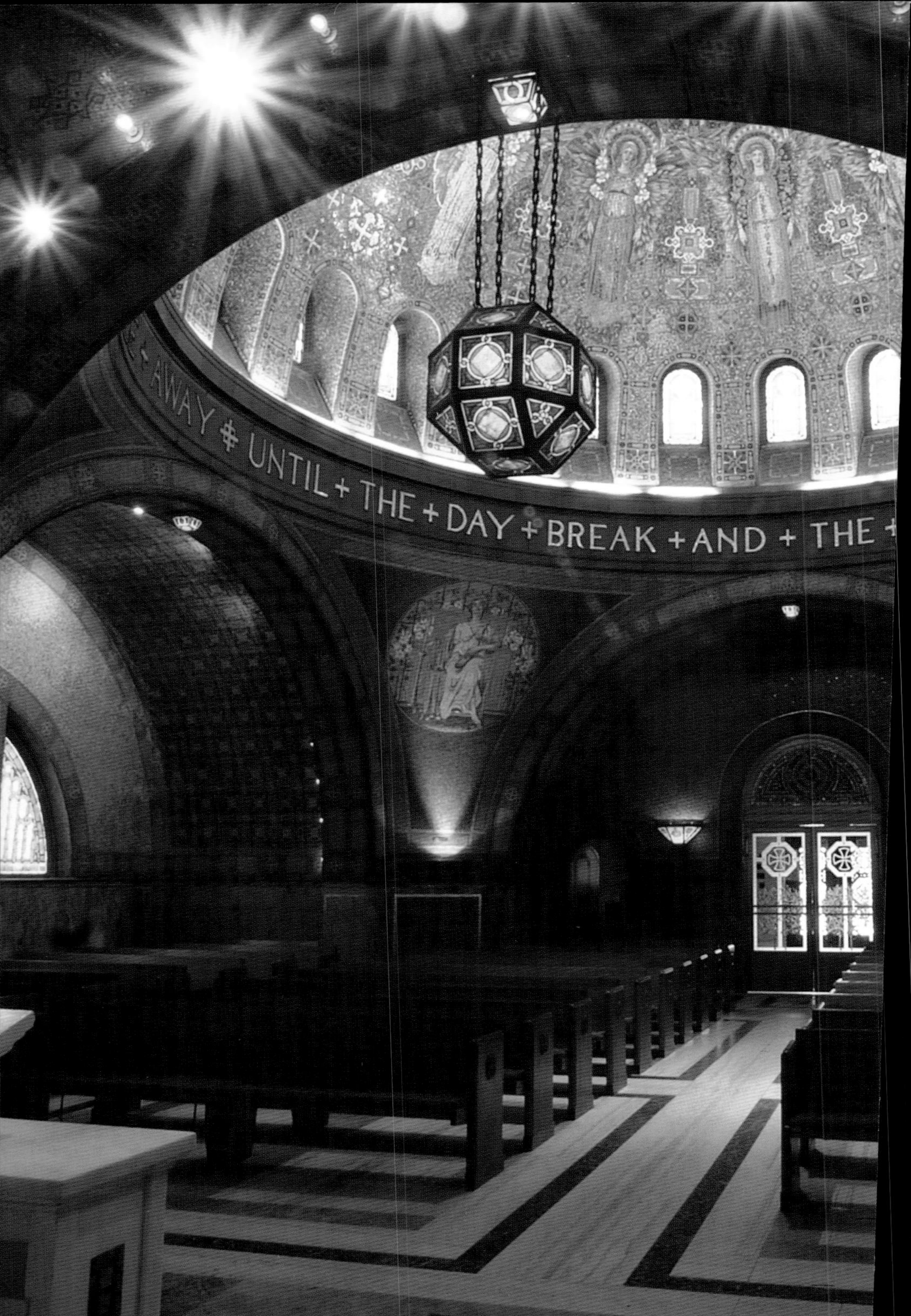
AWAY + UNTIL + THE + DAY + BREAK + AND + THE +

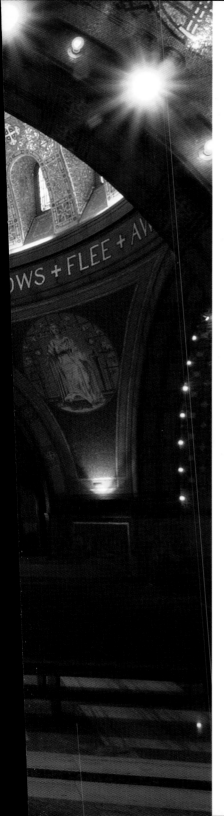

Lakewood Memorial Chapel

Modeled after the Haghia Sophia Church in Istanbul, Turkey, the chapel's stunning interior is decorated with 10 million pieces of marble, colored stone and glass. Prominent architect Harry "Wild" Jones designed the round Byzantine Romanesque-style chapel, which was completed in 1910.

Landmark Center

Famous for its castle-like appearance, Landmark Center is one of St. Paul's most distinctive buildings. Once a federal courthouse and post office, Landmark Center now houses many of the city's premier arts and cultural organizations.

Lock and Dam No. 1

Also known as the Ford Dam, Lock and Dam No. 1 is part of the "Stairway of Water" that allows a navigation channel along the Mississippi River from the Twin Cities to the Gulf of Mexico. An observation deck is open daily from April to November.

Loring Park

Centrally located by downtown Minneapolis, the Basilica and Walker Art Center, the 35-acre park attracts thousands of visitors, including fans of its "Music and Movies in the Park" series.

Mall of America

The nation's largest retail and entertainment destination under one roof, Mall of America encompasses 500-some stores, a 7-acre theme park, a 1.2-million-gallon aquarium and a wedding chapel. It draws 40 million visitors annually—more than Disneyland, Graceland and the Grand Canyon combined.

Marjorie McNeely Conservatory ➤

This half-acre Victorian garden under glass is among the last of its kind in America. Opened in 1915, the conservatory includes century-old palm plants, five seasonal flower shows a year and a new two-story rainforest exhibit. Located adjacent to the Como Zoo, the conservatory is open 365 days a year; admission is free.

Mary Tyler Moore Statue

Tossing her tam-o'-shanter cap in the air, the 8-foot-tall bronze statue honors actress Mary Tyler Moore and her beloved TV character. The statue stands at the corner of 7th Street and Nicollet Mall in downtown Minneapolis, the same spot where Moore joyfully tossed her tam in the show's opening credits.

Metro Transit Hiawatha Line

Built at a cost of $715 million, the Hiawatha line offers fast and efficient light rail service to 17 stations along a 12-mile route between downtown Minneapolis and the Mall of America, with stops at the Humphrey and Lindbergh air terminals.

Mickey's Diner

A St. Paul icon since 1939, Mickey's Diner has been featured in Hollywood films including *Jingle All The Way, Mighty Ducks* and *Prairie Home Companion*. Always open for business, the streamlined Moderne Art Deco diner has just four booths and a 17-seat counter.

Mill City Museum

Rising nine stories above the courtyard ruins of the Washburn A Mill, which was closed in 1965 and destroyed by a fire in 1991, this museum showcases Minneapolis as the flour milling capital of the world between 1880-1930.

Mill Ruins Park ➤

The centerpiece of the revitalization of Minneapolis' historic West Side Milling District, this 10-acre park exposes the ruins of historic water-powered flour mills.

Minneapolis Aquatennial

Held the third full week of July, this annual festival draws nearly 1 million people each year. Popular Aquatennial events include the Sailing Regatta, Milk Carton Boat Race and Torchlight Parade.

MINNEAPOLIS PUBLIC LIBRARY
CENTRAL LIBRARY

Minneapolis Central Library

Designed by world-renowned architect Caesar Pelli and completed in 2006, the dazzling new state-of-the-art Central Library is home to over 3 million books, magazines, pictures and other documents.

Minneapolis City Hall

An architectural treasure, Minneapolis City Hall features
a five-story rotunda and a clock with a face larger than
that of London's famous Big Ben.

Minneapolis Farmers Market

Open seven days a week from early spring until the first mid-November, this farmers' market located at Lyndale and Glenwood Avenues near downtown Minneapolis has been offering the finest foods, flowers and staples to loyal patrons since 1938.

Minneapolis Institute of Arts

Founded in 1883, this world-renowned
facility is home to permanent collections
of paintings by European masters, Asian
antiquities and more than 100,000 objects
of art. Admission is free of charge.

◄ Minneapolis Sculpture Garden

The 55-foot Spoonbridge and Cherry dominates this sculpture garden, the largest such park in America. Across from the Walker Art Center, the outdoor gallery holds more than 40 examples of modern three-dimensional art.

Minneapolis-St. Paul International Airport

Serving more than 36 million travelers a year, the nation's 12th-largest airport handles more than 1,150 commercial flights a day. Its two terminals are named for famous Minnesotans—aviator Charles Lindbergh and politician Hubert Humphrey.

Minnehaha Depot

Nicknamed the "Princess Depot" for its elaborate detailing, this small, Victorian-style building was once the major gateway for tourists who arrived from Minneapolis, St. Paul and Fort Snelling by train and later by streetcar.

Minnehaha Park and Falls

Henry Wadsworth Longfellow's 1853 poem, *Song of Hiawatha*, brought national fame to Minnehaha Falls, which continues to be one of the Twin Cities' most popular recreation areas.

Minnesota Harvest

Open daily year-round and one of America's premier apple orchards—with more than 33,000 trees covering 278 acres—Minnesota Harvest grows over 50 varieties of apples. Visitors can pick their own apples, ride horses and enjoy a seasonal corn maze.

Minnesota History Center

Housed within the Minnesota History Center is the state's largest collection of books, magazines, newspapers, documents, maps, images and artifacts relative to the history of Minnesota's cities, people, business and government. The center also offers state-of-the-art library services, plus permanent and temporary exhibits.

Minnesota Landscape Arboretum

USA Today named the University of Minnesota's arboretum in
Chaska as one of the 10 best botanical gardens in America.

Minnesota State Capitol ➤

Designed by celebrated St. Paul architect Cass Gilbert and completed in 1905 at
a cost of $4.5 million, Minnesota's premier public building was modeled after St.
Peter's Basilica in Rome. Situated above the main entrance is the famed Quadriga, a
team of four gilded stallions symbolizing earth, fire, wind and water.

Minnesota State Fair

Held annually during the 12 days preceding and ending on Labor Day, the "Great Minnesota Get-Together" is famous for its wide variety of food, exhibits and big-name entertainment. Drawing more than 1.5 million visitors each year, it is one of the largest fairs in North America.

Minnesota Twins

The first professional baseball team to be named for a state rather than a city, the Twins have won two World Series championships, in 1987 and 1991.

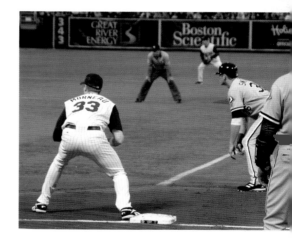

Minnesota Vikings

Established in 1961 and named to reflect the Nordic heritage of many state residents, the Vikings have been a dominant force in the NFL, winning their division 16 times between 1968-2000. Team fans are among the most colorful and energetic in the NFL.

Minnesota Zoo

Over 2,300 animals and 400 species are residents of this 500-acre zoo, which is divided into five themed areas. Open year-round, the zoo also features a 1.5-mile monorail, IMAX theater and amphitheater.

St. Paul skyline over the Mississippi River

Mystic Lake Casino Hotel

With a circular design symbolizing the four seasons, four compass points and four cycles of life, Mystic Lake is among the largest, most successful Indian-owned casinos in the country.

Nicollet Island

The geographic and historic center of Minneapolis since the 1850s, Nicollet Island is a 48-acre sliver of land surrounded by the Mississippi River and home to a small enclave of historic Victorian homes, a park and local high school.

Nicollet Mall

Designed for pedestrians, buses and taxis, the gently curving Nicollet Mall stretches for 12 blocks through the heart of downtown Minneapolis and passes by some of the city's most popular and upscale stores, restaurants and entertainment venues.

Northrop Memorial Auditorium

Known as the "Carnegie Hall of the Midwest" when it opened in 1928,
this neoclassical building, designed by famed St. Paul architect Clarence
Johnston, was named in honor of the University's second and longest-
serving president, Cyrus Northrop.

Oliver H. Kelly Farm ➤

A 189-acre living history site and working farm depicting Minnesota farm life in
the mid-1800s, the site was named in honor of one of the founders of the National
Grange, the country's foremost agricultural fraternal organization.

Orchestra Hall

Home to the world-renowned Minnesota Orchestra, Orchestra
Hall is one of the most acoustically acclaimed music venues in
the world. More than 12 million people have attended over 5,500
performances since the facility opened in 1974.

Ordway Center for the Performing Arts

Named in honor of Lucius P. Ordway, St. Paul entrepreneur and early investor and officer in 3M, the theater opened in 1985 and is a major venue for touring Broadway productions as well as local musical, orchestra and opera performances. Internationally known St. Paul architect Benjamin Thompson designed the distinctive building with its three-level windowed lobby.

Orpheum Theatre

Opened in 1921 as a vaudeville and silent movie house, the historic downtown Minneapolis theater was renovated in 1993 and has hosted featured performances by top-name entertainers and touring Broadway productions such as *Annie, The Lion King* and others.

Our Lady of Lourdes Church

Built between 1854-1857 of limestone quarried from nearby Nicollet Island, this is the oldest Minneapolis church in continuous use. The church was designated a U.S. historic landmark in 1934 and it is the first parish in America named in honor of Our Lady of Lourdes.

Peavey Plaza ➤

Located adjacent to Orchestra Hall and the Nicollet Mall, this city-owned, terraced plaza is the site of many free public concerts, festivals and rallies.

◄ Rice Park

Surrounded by the Central Library, Landmark Center, St. Paul Hotel and the Ordway Theater, this popular public square has been the site of frequent community events, rallies, weddings and celebrations. During the holiday season, the park is transformed into a winter wonderland of illuminated trees and sculptures.

St. Anthony Falls Lock and Dam

During the shipping season, 10-12 barges a day bypass St. Anthony Falls via the northernmost lock facility on the Mississippi River. A public observation deck is located at the site and guided tours are available.

St. Paul RiverCentre

Located adjacent to the Xcel Energy Center, RiverCentre is St. Paul's state-of-the-art convention, special event, concert and entertainment facility.

St. Paul Saints

One of 12 teams in the American Association of Independent Baseball, the St. Paul Saints attract sellout crowds for their lively outdoor games, which feature zany promotions and reasonable ticket prices.

et over the Minneapolis skyline

St. Paul Winter Carnival

Held during a 10-day period ending on the first Sunday in February, the St. Paul Winter Carnival is the largest winter festival in the country and features city-wide events including parades, ice and snow sculptures, sporting events, fireworks and a treasure hunt.

Science Museum of Minnesota

Built into the bluffs overlooking the Mississippi River, this world-class museum features permanent interactive exhibits about fossils and dinosaurs, the human body and the Mississippi River, plus an Omnitheater and temporary gallery for major traveling exhibits.

Sibley House Historic Site

Minnesota's first governor, Henry
H. Sibley, used his six-room
limestone house in Mendota as the
official governor's residence from
1858 to 1862.

State Theatre

In addition to being a popular venue for vaudeville, movies, stage, plays and concerts, this opulent 2,150-seat Italian Renaissance theater was also the site of the world premier of *Grumpy Old Men*.

Stone Arch Bridge ➤

Built across the Mississippi River by railroad baron James J. Hill in 1883, this 2,100-foot curvilinear bridge with 23 arches closed to trains in 1978 and re-opened to pedestrians and bikers in 1994.

Summit Avenue

This fashionable, 5-mile-long, tree-lined boulevard is the longest remaining stretch of residential Victorian architecture in America and passes by the Governor's Mansion plus the homes of railroad tycoon James J. Hill and author F. Scott Fitzgerald.

40	**GOLFING**	
41	**GRAND ROUNDS NATIONAL SCENIC BYWAY**	www.minneapolisparks.org
42	**GUTHRIE THEATER**	818 South 2nd Street, Minneapolis, MN 55415; 612-377-2224; www.guthrietheater.org
43	**HARRIET ISLAND**	Plato Boulevard and West Water Street, St. Paul, MN 55107 ; 651-266-6400; www.nps.gov/miss
44	**HISTORIC FORT SNELLING**	Junction of Highways 55 & 5 one mile east of airport; 612-726-1171; www.mnhs.org/fortsnelling
46	**HISTORIC MURPHY'S LANDING**	2187 East Highway 101, Shakopee, MN 55379; 763-694-7784; www.murphyslanding.com
47	**HOLIDAZZLE** *Typically runs through the holiday season*	Nicollet Mall, Minneapolis, MN; www.holidazzle.com
48	**HUBERT H. HUMPHREY METRODOME**	501 Chicago Avenue , Minneapolis, MN 55415; 612-332-0386; www.msfc.com
50	**JACKSON STREET ROUNDHOUSE**	193 Pennsylvania Avenue East, St. Paul, MN 55130; 651-228-0263; www.mtmuseum.org
52	**JAMES J. HILL HOUSE**	240 Summit Avenue, St. Paul, MN 55102; 651-297-2555; www.mnhs.org
53	**JOHN H. STEVENS HOUSE**	4901 Minnehaha Avenue South, Minneapolis, MN; 612-722-2220; www.johnhstevenshouse.org
54	**JONATHAN PADELFORD**	Harriet Island, St. Paul, MN 55107; 651-227-1100; www.riverrides.com
56	**LAKE CALHOUN**	3000 Calhoun Pkwy., Minneapolis, MN 55408; 612-230-6400; www.minneapolisparks.org
57	**LAKE HARRIET**	43rd Street West and East Lake Harriet Parkway , Minneapolis, MN; 612-230-6475; www.minneapolisparks.org
58	**LAKE HARRIET-LYNDALE PARK ROSE GARDEN**	4124 Roseway Road, Minneapolis, MN 55409; 612-370-4838; www.minneapolisparks.com
60	**LAKEWOOD MEMORIAL CHAPEL**	3600 Hennepin Avenue South, Minneapolis, MN 55408; 612-822-2171; www.lakewoodcemetery.com
62	**LANDMARK CENTER**	75 West Fifth Street, St. Paul, MN 55102; 651-292-3233; www.landmarkcenter.org
63	**LOCK AND DAM NO. 1**	5000 West River Parkway south of Ford Parkway Bridge, Minneapolis, MN; 612-724-2971; www.nps.gov/miss
64	**LORING PARK**	1382 Willow Street, Minneapolis, MN 55403; 612-370-4929; www.minneapolisparks.org
65	**MALL OF AMERICA**	Crossroads of Interstate 494 & Hwy 77, Bloomington, MN; 952-883-8800; www.mallofamerica.com
66	**MARJORIE MCNEELEY CONSERVATORY**	1225 Estabrook Drive, St. Paul, MN 55103; 651-487-8200; www.comozooconservatory.org
68	**MARY TYLER MOORE STATUE**	Corner of 7th Street & Hennepin Avenue, Minneapolis, MN
69	**METRO TRANSIT HIAWATHA LINE**	Downtown Minneapolis to Mall of America; 612-373-3333; www.metrotransit.org/rail
70	**MICKEY'S DINER**	36 Seventh Street West, St. Paul, MN 55102; 651-222-5633
71	**MILL CITY MUSEUM**	704 South Second Street, Minneapolis, MN 55401; 612-341-7555; www.millcitymuseum.org
72	**MILL RUINS PARK**	Portland Avenue & West River Parkway, Minneapolis, MN; 612-313-7793; www.minneapolisparks.org
	MINNEAPOLIS AQUATENNIAL *Typically runs the third full week in July*	Various venues throughout Minneapolis; www.aquatennial.org

76	**MINNEAPOLIS CENTRAL LIBRARY**	300 Nicollet Mall, Minneapolis, MN 55401; 612-630-6000; www.mpls.lib.mn.us/central.asp
77	**MINNEAPOLIS CITY HALL**	350 South 5th Street, Minneapolis, MN 55415; 612-673-3000; www.ci.minneapolis.mn.us
78	**MINNEAPOLIS FARMERS MARKET**	312 East Lyndale Avenue North, Minneapolis, MN 55405; 612-333-1718; www.mplsfarmersmarket.com
79	**MINNEAPOLIS INSTITUTE OF ARTS**	2400 Third Avenue South, Minneapolis, MN 55404; 612-870-3000; www.artsmia.org
80	**MINNEAPOLIS SCULPTURE GARDEN**	Vineland Place, across from the Walker Art Center, Minneapolis, MN 55403; http://garden.walkerart.org
82	**MINNEAPOLIS-ST. PAUL INTERNATIONAL AIRPORT**	Lindbergh Terminal, 4300 Glumack Drive, St. Paul, MN 55111; 612-726-5555; www.mspairport.com/msp; Humphrey Terminal, 7150 Humphrey Drive, Minneapolis, MN 55450; 612-726-5800
83	**MINNEHAHA DEPOT**	In Minnehaha Park near Highway 55 and Minnehaha Parkway, Minneapolis, MN; 651-228-0263; www.mnhs.org
84	**MINNEHAHA PARK AND FALLS**	4801 Minnehaha Avenue South, Minneapolis, MN 55417; 612-230-6400; www.minneapolisparks.org
85	**MINNESOTA HARVEST**	8251 Old Highway 169 Boulevard, Jordan, MN 55352; 952-492-7753; www.minnesotaharvest.net
86	**MINNESOTA HISTORY CENTER**	345 West Kellogg Boulevard, St. Paul, MN 55102; 651-259-3000; www.mnhs.org
87	**MINNESOTA LANDSCAPE ARBORETUM**	3675 Arboretum Drive, Chaska, MN 55318; 952-443-1400; www.arboretum.umn.edu
88	**MINNESOTA STATE CAPITOL**	345 Kellogg Boulevard , St. Paul, MN 55102; 651-259-3000; www.mnhs.org/places/sites/msc
90	**MINNESOTA STATE FAIR**	1265 Snelling Avenue North, St. Paul, MN 55108; 651-288-4400; www.mnstatefair.org
91	**MINNESOTA TWINS**	501 Chicago Avenue, Minneapolis, MN 55415; 612-338-9467; www.minnesota.twins.mlb.com
92	**MINNESOTA VIKINGS**	Games held at Hubert H. Humphrey Metrodome; www.vikings.com
93	**MINNESOTA ZOO**	13000 Zoo Boulevard, Apple Valley, MN 55124; 952-431-9200; www.mnzoo.com
94	**MYSTIC LAKE CASINO**	2400 Mystic lake Boulevard, Prior Lake, MN 55372; 952-445-9000; www.mysticlake.com
95	**NICOLLET ISLAND**	40 Power Street, Minneapolis, MN 55401; 612 230-6400; www.minneapolisparks.org
96	**NICOLLET MALL**	Nicollet Ave. between Washington & 13th Avenues South, Minneapolis, MN
97	**NORTHROP MEMORIAL AUDITORIUM**	84 Church Street, Minneapolis, MN 55455; 612-625-6600; www1.umn.edu/umato
98	**OLIVER H. KELLY FARM**	2.5 miles southeast of downtown Elk River on US Hwy 10; 763-441-6896; www.mnhs.org
100	**ORCHESTRA HALL**	1111 Nicollet Avenue, Minneapolis, MN 55403; 612-371-5656 www.minnesotaorchestra.org
101	**ORDWAY CENTER FOR THE PERFORMING ARTS**	345 Washington Street, St. Paul, MN 55102; 651-224-4222; www.ordway.org
102	**ORPHEUM THEATRE**	910 Hennepin Avenue, Minneapolis, MN 55403; 612-339-7007;. www.hennepintheatredistrict.org
103	**OUR LADY OF LOURDES CHURCH**	1 Lourdes Place, Minneapolis, MN 55414; 612-379-2259; www.ourladyoflourdesmn.com

104	**PEAVEY PLAZA**	1111 Nicollet Mall, Minneapolis, MN 55403; 612-371-5693; www.minnesotaorchestra.org
106	**RAPTOR CENTER**	1920 Fitch Avenue, St. Paul, MN 55108; 612-624-4745; www.raptor.cvm.umn.edu
107	**RICE PARK**	Washington Street and West Fourth Street, St. Paul, MN
108	**ST. ANTHONY FALLS LOCK AND DAM**	1 Portland Avenue , Minneapolis, MN 55401; 612-333-5336; www.nps.gov/miss
110	**ST. ANTHONY FALLS WATER POWER PARK**	Downtown Minneapolis on the Mississippi River at St. Anthony Falls, Minneapolis, MN; 800-895-4999
111	**ST. PAUL CITY HALL AND RAMSEY COUNTY COURTHOUSE**	15 West Kellogg Boulevard, St. Paul, MN 55102; www.stpaul.gov
112	**SAINT PAUL HOTEL**	350 Market Street, St. Paul, MN 55102; 651-292-9292; www.stpaulhotel.com
113	**ST. PAUL RIVERCENTRE**	175 West Kellogg Boulevard, St. Paul, MN 55102; 651-265-4800; www.rivercentre.org
114	**ST. PAUL SAINTS**	1771 Energy Park Drive, St. Paul, MN 55108; 651-644-6659; www.saintsbaseball.com
116	**ST. PAUL WINTER CARNIVAL** *Typically begins the fourth week in January*	Various venues throughout St. Paul; www.winter-carnival.com
117	**SCIENCE MUSEUM OF MINNESOTA**	120 West Kellogg Boulevard, St. Paul, MN 55102; 651-221-9444; www.smm.org
118	**SIBLEY HOUSE HISTORIC SITE**	Downtown Mendota on Sibley , Memorial Highway, Mendota, MN; 651-452-1596; www.mnhs.org
119	**STATE THEATER**	805 Hennepin Avenue, Minneapolis, MN 55402; 612-339-7007; www.hennepintheatredistrict.org
120	**STONE ARCH BRIDGE**	Intersection of West River Road and Portland Avenue in downtown Minneapolis , Minneapolis, MN; 651-296-6126; www.nps.gov/miss
122	**SUMMIT AVENUE**	St. Paul, MN
123	**TARGET CENTER**	600 First Avenue North, Minneapolis, MN 55403; 612-673-1300; www.targetcenter.com
24	**THEODORE WIRTH PARK**	1339 Theodore Wirth Pkwy., Minneapolis, MN 55411 ; 612-230-6400; www.minneapolisparks.org
24	**THEODORE WIRTH HOUSE**	3954 Bryant Avenue South, Minneapolis, MN 55409; www.ci.minneapolis.mn.us
26	**TWIN CITY MODEL RAILROAD MUSEUM**	1021 Bandana Boulevard East # 222 , St. Paul, MN 55108; 651-647-9628; www.tcmrm.org
27	**UNIVERSITY OF MINNESOTA**	Office of Admissions, 240 Williamson Hall, 231 Pillsbury Drive S.E., Minneapolis, MN 55455; 800-752-1000; www1.umn.edu/twincities
28	**UPTOWN**	Lake Street & Hennepin Avenue, Minneapolis, MN
29	**VALLEYFAIR**	1 Valleyfair Drive, Shakopee, MN 55379; 952-445-6500; www.valleyfair.com
30	**WABASHA STREET CAVES**	215 Wabasha Street, So. St. Paul, MN 55107; 651-292-1220; www.wabashastreetcaves.com
2	**WALKER ART CENTER**	1750 Hennepin Avenue, Minneapolis, MN 55403; 612-375-7600; www.walkerart.org
3	**XCEL ENERGY CENTER**	175 West Kellogg Boulevard, St. Paul, MN 55102; 651-265-4800; www.xcelenergycenter.com

About the Author

An avid photographer for more than 40 years, Gregg Felsen is blessed with an intuitive eye for composition and the ability to transform visual encounters with the world into memorable and lasting images, and has successfully turned his avocation into his vocation.

Felsen concentrates his photographic efforts on sensitivity and creatively captures the unique characteristics of people, places, events, flowers and plants, scenic landscapes, vintage motor cars, historical sites, tombstones and cemeteries, plus architectural and interior design projects of builders, developers, decorators and realtors. Felsen is a member of the American Society of Media Photographers, the North American Nature Photography Association and the Professional Photographers of America.

"Most photographers work very hard at capturing the moment," says Felsen. "But I am always looking for something a little different, a little more artistic than the standard shot. I'm trying to capture images that are unique and which will separate my work from that of other photographers."

You can check out Gregg Felsen's entire catalog of images at his website: www.greggfelsenphotography.com.